Me Again

Good Times With
Family & Friends

TOM CRIBBIN

Story Advisor: Paddy Cunningham Schauteet

Editors: Krystal Butler
    Valerie Cairns
    Marc Giampietri
    Tom St. Amand

Proof Reader: Adriana Vani

Cover Design & Illustration:
    Michael Slotwinski

Me Again
ISBN: 978-0-9683302-3-4

Although the enclosed stories are based on actual experiences, many surnames were either omitted or modified for publication purposes.

First Printing: October 2009
Printed in Canada

Contact information: Tom Cribbin
    www.tomcribbin.com

PREFACE

Family and friends are the themes throughout this book. I have established a good rapport with the regular readers of my collection of humourous adventures. Furthermore, I have made some long-lasting friendships as a result of selling my books directly to people. _Me Again_ immediately came to mind as the title for this fifth book. Every few years, my loyal readers have come to expect a knock on their door asking if they would like to read another book from me. I mystify some customers as I appear at their doors just days after my name surfaces in one of their dinnertime conversations. It is comforting when people stop me in the store or at a sporting event and ask me when more stories will be ready for them to read. Customers are, I hope, happy with my story telling.

I am thankful to those people who had the patience to listen to my speech cadence and pronunciation as I attempted to sell them a copy of my books. Individuals who were quite skeptical of me when I first introduced myself to them are now among my most loyal readers. Gradually, I am changing the attitudes of individuals who were the foundation for some stories in previous books. This continues to inspire me to continue writing about my adventures.

The interpersonal relationships I have with new and existing customers in _Me Again_ are definitely offbeat and unusual. As you will read, some stories have nothing to do with my speech difference, but rather with everyday occurrences, which we all encounter. I am amazed at the wide diversity of topics discussed when I appear on a doorstep with my book. You can believe me when I say I discuss topics that I would not have imagined. One particular story will definitely garner differing responses between males and females.

I hope you will find my stories in *Me Again* humourous, interesting and entertaining about my interpersonal relationships with family and friends. A few experiences might even cause your eyebrow to rise or your jaw to drop as they did with me.

Tom Cribbin

I dedicate this story to

Judy Gould

FRIGHTENING HEIGHTS

When I was a child, my affliction with cerebral palsy did not preclude me from being mischievous. Just like any other child, I found myself in typical situations. My family devoted many Sunday afternoons to visiting relatives. My aunt and her family lived for a time at the trailer park on London Line, then known as Highway 7. In the 1960's, this was the main road to London prior to the construction of the four-lane 402 Highway. After I visited with the adults, Allan and Shelley, two of my cousins, and I went outside to play catch. Allan saw an abandoned cabin in the far distance, which intrigued him, and eventually we made it to this structure for a closer look. The dilapidated cabin, with its flat roof, sat in a heavily weeded field where the four-lane highway now crosses the landscape.

My cousins and I checked out the cabin and its immediate surroundings. When Allan saw a ladder at the back of the cabin, he climbed it quickly and reached its rooftop. He shouted from the roof, coaxing his sister and me to join him. I reluctantly agreed and my two cousins helped me to navigate the steps on the wobbly ladder. Allan was ahead of me on the ladder, while Shelley was behind, to steady my climb. The climb might have had only six or seven simple steps to reach the top; but, for me, the climb was a somewhat challenging one to achieve. Once I reached the top step, Allan pulled me to the safety of the flat roof and he did likewise for his sister. While atop the roof, I remained near the centre for fear of falling to the ground.

I discovered the most exciting aspect of being on a rooftop was the adventure of actually climbing the ladder. As soon as sitting on the roof satisfied our curiosity, we thought about returning to my aunt's trailer. The time was now late afternoon, we were hungry and thirsty, and, more importantly, we needed to return soon, so we would not be in trouble.

Allan climbed down the ladder easily, as did Shelley. While I watched my two cousins navigate the steps downward, I doubted my own ability to make it safely to the ground. As I witnessed them step down the ladder, I realized I would not be able to see where to place my feet on the ladder's steps. This revelation scared me. I repeatedly yelled and screamed to Allan and Shelley,

| | I can't get down! I can't get down! I can't get down! Help me! Someone, please help me! |
| Allan: | Okay, I will go and get some help. |

Allan quickly ran back to the trailer where he told everybody about my predicament. He sought help from my other cousin, Tim, to bring me down from the roof.

About thirty minutes elapsed before Shelley and I heard a sound similar to the engine of a motorbike that drew ever so close. With Allan was Tim, who was carrying Allan as a passenger on his mini-bike.

Tim: What seems to be the problem?
Tom: I can't get down. I'm scared that I will fall.

Tim thought of an idea; then he and Allan came onto the roof.

Tim: Allan and I will help you down. Tommy, don't worry, we won't let you fall.

Tim guided my foot carefully onto every step until I reached the ground. Allan followed me down the steps. After I made it to the ground safely, Tim gave me a ride to the trailer on his mini-bike while Allan and Shelley ran beside us.

During the remainder of my childhood, I stayed away from climbing ladders, any abandoned buildings and trees around our neighbourhood. I definitely learned the lesson that climbing was not, and is still not, my forte.

Years later, I remembered the abandoned cabin episode when I was on a school excursion to New York City. My classmates and I visited the magnificent Statue of Liberty on Liberty Island in New York's harbour during a day of unbearable heat. The tour guide told us about the history, the significance, and the grandeur of the statue. Additionally, we learned that tourists had the opportunity to climb to the crown of Lady Liberty via an interior winding staircase. A classmate, who also happened to be a neighbourhood friend, asked me,

> Will you be able to make it all the way to the crown in this heat?

I responded confidently by saying,

> I won't have any problem with getting to the top.

Soon, we found ourselves in the line to trek up the Statue of Liberty to her crown.

The heat permeated the interior of the statue and, as a consequence, made the 354-step climb from the pedestal to her crown *that* much more daunting. Once I reached the top, I quickly scanned the skyline and then immediately headed down another 354 steps to the ground.

The climb to the Statue of Liberty's crown was a great feat to accomplish at that moment, but I would not attempt it again.

Tom Cribbin

I dedicate this story to

Mr. & Mrs. Ian Macdonald

NICKNAME SIGNIFICANCE

Each one of us has had nicknames at different stages in our lives. Such names play an important role in the way in which other people view us. Generally, I am not in favour of nicknames for 'nicknames' sake. Having said this, however, I welcome the nicknames assigned to me by individuals who either have played or currently play a significant role in my life.

Throughout the 1960's and '70's, the _Peanuts_ cartoon strip enjoyed immense popularity among adults and children. This series was very much a social commentary about all our lives as much as it was entertaining. The _Peanuts_ cartoon strip centred around one character, Charlie Brown, the so-called 'underdog' whom everybody rooted for in his many adventures. The premise of this character's existence was his perseverance and motivation. As early as I can remember, my dad sporadically called me 'Charlie Brown'. I have my own assumption of why Dad assigned the 'Charlie Brown' moniker to me. Since I have cerebral palsy, Dad drew a parallel between my persistence and determination and that of the lovable cartoon character.

Dad called me 'Charlie Brown' for motivational reasons. Whenever I threw the ball accurately, Dad would say, "Good throw, Charlie Brown!" Likewise, when it appeared that my cerebral palsy would hinder me from achieving the simplest of goals such as riding a bike, I could count on a lesson from the *Peanuts'* series. Dad would say, "Tommy, keep trying. Eventually, Charlie Brown prevails in his adventures. I have the utmost confidence in your ability."

Following my father's passing, our former parish priest, Father Nick Marro kept the *Peanuts* cartoon strip alive each week in his very engaging homilies. Whenever the priest would relate the *Peanuts* strip to the religious readings, I could expect a nudge and a smile from my mother. It was as though Dad was telling me a story via Father Nick's lips.

Each time a *Peanuts'* Holiday special plays on television, the Charlie Brown character always invokes fond memories of my dad. The 'Charlie Brown' moniker sure was extra-special when Dad called me this endearing name.

After my final two years of grade school enduring some classmates who called me derogatory names because of my cerebral palsy, I entered high school. In my first week of high school, I was walking through the lounge when an older student motioned to me to come over to his table. The student and others introduced themselves as the Grade 13 students. I introduced myself with some trepidation to them. Chris, Jamie and John gave me their names and extended an invitation to stop by their table and say, 'hello'. When I departed the conversation, Chris said, "See you around, Stomping Tom."

Typically in high school, the older grade 13 students paid no attention to the often shy, grade 9 students. Therefore, I was feeling very good about myself because not only did I meet the grade 13 students, but most everyone welcomed me with open arms. I was the talk of the school. The difference in the attitudes of the high school students and my former grade school classmates was like day and night. My own attitude about my cerebral palsy began to mature. By calling me 'Stomping Tom', the grade 13 students viewed my gait as a positive characteristic and, therefore, I accepted the moniker. After all, I was not about to argue with Chris, Jamie and John — members of the senior football team — about the imposed nickname for me.

Variations of the 'Stomping Tom' name remained with me throughout my high school years. Yet, the nickname did not hold as great a significance for me as it did when Chris, Jamie and John called out Stomping Tom.

The 'Charlie Brown' and 'Stomping Tom' monikers were from my childhood and high school years respectively. People at differing points in my life bestowed these two nicknames upon me for different reasons in my formative years.

My given name is Thomas, which was also the name of my father and my grandfather. As with names from my generation, parents would often shorten the given name to a less formal one such as Tom or Tommy. When I was a child, my parents called me Tommy to distinguish me from my father and everyone else followed their lead even into adulthood. Recently, I met Mrs. Mussio, one of my teachers in elementary school, and, subsequently, told her about my books. She commented, "Although the name on your book says 'Tom Cribbin', you will always remain Tommy to me." When she bought one of my books, I signed it as Tommy Cribbin. I realize I am still Tommy to some relatives and to select people from my past. That is fine with me!

A nickname bestowed upon me by people of significance indicates total acceptance and perfection in their eyes, minds and hearts.

Tom Cribbin

I dedicate this story to

Don & Eleanor Buchser

WORRISOME MOM

Despite having cerebral palsy, my parents had always placed me in age-appropriate situations. When I was young, my mom and dad raised me as if I was like any other child. Many parents pamper their disabled children by treating them as if they are younger than their actual age. Mom and Dad did not believe in this philosophy of babying a 'disabled' child. My mother continued this age-appropriate rearing of me even after she unfortunately became a widow at the young age of 44. It was the year of my dad's passing that I gave my mother a real scare.

I was attending a school assembly in grade seven when the school principal asked me to come with him. When called by the principal unexpectedly, I obviously had a confused expression on my face. In the principal's office was a representative from the Focus Rehab Treatment Centre who was to take me to the Guildwood Inn to attend the Centre's Christmas party. I explained to the principal's office that my mother had not granted permission to me to attend. Feigning a smile, I reluctantly but obediently, went to the party with the centre's and the school's permission.

My mother had discussed with me just a few months before, and I agreed, that I was too old to receive a gift from Santa Claus at those parties. As a result of this conversation, Mom declined the invitation for my attendance at the Christmas party when Focus Rehab contacted her.

Earlier that year, the Focus Rehab Centre had undergone some administrative changes by hiring a new executive director. The long-time executive director had retired at the beginning of the summer and the Board of Directors hired a much younger person to administer the evolving organization.

It worried Mom when I failed to come home for lunch that day. She phoned some neighbours to determine my whereabouts. A friend told his mother that the principal's office had pulled me away from the Christmas assembly for some reason. Mom telephoned the school to inquire about me. The school informed her that the Focus Rehab Centre came and took Tommy to their Christmas party as they had done in previous years. My teacher wondered about the Christmas party as I had a bewildered expression on my face indicating my uncertainty. At that point, my mother drove to the Guildwood Inn and waited for me until the party's end. As with many instances, Mom handled the situation with grace and class. She thanked the organizers for showing her son a good time.

On the drive home from the party, my mother calmly and lovingly explained to me that I had given her a real scare. She reiterated that I was not to go places without having prior permission from her. Since my sister was away at university, it was primarily Mom and I.

We made a promise not to make the other worry unnecessarily if at all possible.

As a result of this incident and a few other misguided actions, the Board of Directors dismissed the newly appointed Executive Director at Focus Rehab after only a few months on the job. The school established a new protocol of having a written and signed note from the parent for any outside appointments or events. When a third party is providing the transportation, then the provider must also show signed declaration from the parent allowing the child to leave the school premises with that provider.

I rarely saw my mother irate over too many situations in her life. If she thought either one of her two children was in some circumstance of potential danger, then Mom handled the situation in a firm, swift and dignified manner.

Tom Cribbin

15

I dedicate this story to

Mike Thornton & Tiffany Clarke

JUST LIKE "NUMBER 4"

The weekend road hockey game filled the spare time of my neighbourhood buddies and me, as did other rituals during my youth. Since I could not balance on skates, I was in my element when my neighbourhood buddies played a game of road hockey. Each weekend afternoon, we would gather at the south end of the street to emulate our heroes from the NHL. Most of my friends idolized players from the Toronto Maple Leafs with the exception of myself. During these hockey games, I pretended to be like the star defenceman of the Boston Bruins, number 4, Bobby Orr.

A heated rivalry developed between the boys from the opposite sides of the street. Coincidentally, we Catholic kids all resided on one side whereas the non-Catholics lived on the other. Consequently, the selection of the teams was easy. I might be a tad biased in saying that my team had the best players. Our team was comprised of Carlo at centre, with his energetic attitude and Rocco on wing with his unorthodox sticks. The Lange boys made their contribution to the hockey games by providing an additional spot on the wing and on defence. The last spot was mine on defence. I had a very powerful but mostly inaccurate slap shot. My teammates considered my determination to score a goal with my powerful slap shot as their secret weapon.

Our competition for these classic ball hockey games included the two Kevins, Darren, Matt, and either Danny or Al. Then, Joe, outfitted in his goaltender's equipment from head to toe, was our competitor's goaltender. For purposes of the road hockey games, we allowed Joe to convert from his Catholic upbringing to be a member of the rival team. Joe proved himself to be an excellent goaltender against the relentless players from my team. Since our team had no actual goaltender, the other defenceman and I rotated the roles of protecting the net.

Each Saturday and Sunday, where the street had a slight incline, the same group from the neighbourhood would gather for our marathon game of road hockey. The opposition's net was at the edge of the incline so each player had the opportunity to shoot a rolling ball. If a defenceman could time the shot as the rolling ball touched the stick's blade, he had a much more powerful and wicked scoring chance. When I launched my booming slap shot, it was either off-target or it was stopped by the opposing goaltender. My role as a defenceman was primarily to pass the ball to players at the forward position to create our team's scoring opportunities on Joe. My objective was to have fun as scoring a goal seemed impossible for me.

However, one afternoon when the ball rolled to me at the defence point, I slapped it with enormous force where the perfect shot found the upper left corner of the net behind Joe. My teammates, the opposing players, and especially myself were in awe that I had finally scored with my booming slap shot. Scoring a goal felt great! Joe admitted that he did not have a chance on my excellent shot.

The unorganized road hockey games provided entertainment and exercise for kids in the neighbourhood. When I scored my goal on Joe, it was as though I had scored the winning goal for hockey's ultimate prize, the Stanley Cup. Whenever I see these friends from the neighbourhood, the tales of the intense road hockey games undoubtedly enter the conversation.

Tom Cribbin

I dedicate this story to

Brian & Cathy Patenaude and Family

TEARY-EYED MOM

S ince the passing of our father in 1973, my sister Cathy and I vowed to make any milestones extra special for our mother. We enjoyed giving Mom astonishing gifts in an unexpected way, which usually made her cry. Cathy and I were planning a very special evening for our mother's fiftieth birthday. My sister and I were thinking of a memorable gift for Mom. We decided upon a gold stickpin to accent her blazers, dresses, and blouses.

While Cathy was home for the Thanksgiving weekend from Queen's University, Mom showed her a figurine that she saw in a jewelry store window at the local mall. Mom liked only those figurines that had a special sentimental meaning for her. The figurine in question was of a boy and his dog that reminded Mom of Sandy, our dog, and me. My mother loved the figurine. Every time Mom and I would go to the mall before Thanksgiving, she would stop by the store window and say to me, "Tom, no one has bought my boy, yet."

Mom and I walked by the jewelry store window a few weeks after the holiday weekend and the figurine was gone. I could see the disappointment etched in my mom's beautiful face. Mom asked the storekeeper if they had moved the figurine to an in-store location and he confirmed the disappointing news that it had been sold. I shared in Mom's disappointment and did not let the eventual surprise slip out of my big mouth.

Despite Cathy's hectic school load at university, she came home for the weekend to celebrate Mom's birthday. My sister surprised Mom as she made reservations from Kingston at the new posh restaurant near Centennial Park for the three of us. Mom looked especially beautiful that evening. She wore a fancy dress, she had her hair styled, and thankfully her Rheumatoid Arthritis was under control. In my opinion, our mother was a very beautiful and stylish woman. Of course, I am biased by my love for her.

The opulent restaurant served French cuisine, had Maître-D's in tuxedos, and provided violin-playing musicians at the tables upon request. The food was delicious and, for such an exclusive eating establishment, the room was well illuminated. We enjoyed a quiet dinner talking, laughing, and reminiscing about Dad. Cathy and I presented Mom with a small gold-wrapped box. Mom knew by the size of the box that it was not her children who had bought 'The Boy and His Dog' figurine. Nevertheless, Mom unwrapped the small box, albeit with a sheepish smile on her face. Mom was very happy with the stickpin. Mom thanked both of us very much for the unusual stickpin in honour of her fiftieth.

Mom and I took Cathy to the station early on Sunday morning so she could board the train back to Kingston. When Cathy boarded the train, she winked at me as to say that Mom's reaction to her birthday gift went exactly as planned.

During the next month, I asked Mom about her Christmas wish list. My mother was the type of person who requested only routine gifts such as a nice sweater, mitts, towels, or a record. She rarely asked Cathy and me for really expensive, decorative items for the house. This particular Christmas was no exception.

Cathy came home for the Christmas Holidays on December 19th. She assisted Mom with baking, last minute shopping, and gift-wrapping. While Mom was at work, my sister and I would finish shopping for Mom's gifts. Cathy and I decided to wrap Mom's big gift, which we had bought on Thanksgiving weekend, in an over-sized box.

It was Christmas morning and, as usual, our living room floor lay scattered with wrapped parcels. Mom spoiled us. After we took turns opening various gifts, Cathy gestured to Mom and told her to unwrap the over-sized box. Mom did not have any clue as to what the large box contained. Cathy and I watched intently while Mom unwrapped her special gift. Mom had this peculiar expression on her face as she looked at the appliance box. Cathy smiled at me and I began to laugh. Mom proceeded to open the appliance box with curiosity and discovered plenty of tissue paper. As she removed some tissue paper, she caught a glimpse of a figurine and began to cry. I had not seen Mom so overwhelmed with any gift as I did with 'The Boy and His Dog' figurine. While tears of joy poured down Mom's face, she exclaimed: "I don't believe it. This lovely figurine is actually mine." When Mom regained her composure, Cathy and I explained to her that we had the figurine since

Thanksgiving weekend. "Rather than giving the figurine to you on your fiftieth birthday, we decided to wait until today to give it to you," remarked my sister. Cathy also said, "It would have been too obvious to give the figurine to you on your birthday. Tom and I wanted to really surprise you by waiting to see your reactions both at the restaurant and today." Still teary-eyed, Mom said, "Thank you ever so much for the gift. It is definitely more beautiful here than in the store window. I just love it, and I love my two kids for becoming wonderful and thoughtful people."

My mother was a gracious woman with a sentimental side. During Mom's life, Cathy and I always enjoyed giving Mom gifts that would entice her to shed a tear or two.

Tom Cribbin

I dedicate this story to

Susan Jones

TWO-BIT FLOYD

I rang the bell of a gray-sided bungalow on Lakeshore Road expecting Dwayne Reynolds, a former neighbour, to answer the door. The man who opened the door resembled my one-time neigbbour in terms of his six-foot height and husky build. We exchanged our names and he gave his name as Floyd. After walking approximately half the length of the city to get to this gray-sided house near Murphy Road, I was disappointed to find that Dwayne had changed addresses. Nevertheless, the opportunity was there for me to introduce my book to Floyd, a potential reader of my stories.

I began the conversation with the following statement to Floyd concerning the whereabouts of Mr. Reynolds.

	You are not Dwayne! Has he moved?
Floyd:	Dwayne moved about a year ago. He is still in the city. I do not have his exact address.
Tom:	That is all right. I know where Dwayne works. I will contact his workplace on Monday.
Floyd:	Are you a friend of his?

23

Tom: We lived in the same neighbourhood when we were young. Dwayne buys a book from me whenever I write a new one.

Floyd called Karen, his wife, to the door to join the conversation. Floyd told his wife that I know Dwayne from my childhood and that he purchases my books.

Karen: What type of books do you write?

Tom: The stories are about the humourous conversations I have with people when I sell my books to them. The underlying theme is my speech difference and the spontaneous reactions from residents towards the way I talk.

Floyd: What made you write these books?

Tom: I had originally planned to write only one book. However, when I began to market it door-to-door, I discovered the potential of more books as people reacted differently to me — from being kind to being absurd. I have the feeling that one of you might say something humourous during this meeting.

Karen: How long have you had your speech difficulty?

Tom: I was born with a condition known as Cerebral Palsy. This affects my pronunciation of words and the fluency of speech.

I allowed Floyd and Karen to preview my latest book.

Karen:	I like the unique way that you displayed the stories.
Tom:	Most of my existing customers have made similar comments about my story telling.
Floyd:	I would even like to read stories in this dialogue format. Would we know any one in your book?
Tom:	No. I modified every name in the book, but I am positive you can see yourselves in some of the stories.

Karen turned to Floyd and said, "Let's buy a copy."

Karen:	What is your asking price for a copy?
Tom:	The price is twenty.
Karen:	I will get you the twenty from my purse.

Floyd tells his wife that he has the money in his pocket. He pulls out a quarter and hands it to me. Then he said jokingly,

> Here are two bits. Tom, you made five cents more than your asking price!

My sarcastic response to Floyd was:

> WOW! Aren't you the most generous person I have ever met?

| Karen: | Don't let my husband rattle you. I know what you meant. Here is a twenty-dollar bill for your book. |

Tom:	Thank you very much, Karen. I should be on my way now. You both are very nice people. I appreciated the laugh that you gave me. I will say 'dollars' after the amount of the book from now on
Floyd:	Karen and I wish you all the best.

.

The meeting of Karen and Floyd was accidental at this particular residence on Lakeshore, and, as the conversation unfolded, ended in a memorable stop during the marketing of my books. After meeting countless people at their doorsteps, I immediately sensed this presentation would be lighthearted. I should not assume that a person understands what is meant in a sentence when I neglect to mention a key word. Although the word 'dollars' is implied, I will remember to include it.

Tom Cribbin

I dedicate this story to

Frank & Gloria Benson

MARILYN'S BABY FAT

One summer evening I was in a quiet community alongside Lake Huron marketing my books to its residents. Like other bedroom communities outside an urban area, the pace of life is slower. I always enjoy marketing my books here, as the residents are welcoming and do not rush me through my brief presentation. Through the years, as a result of marketing my books, people of this community would address me by my name and I would do likewise. As with the many neighbourhoods I visit, occupants of each residence are not always home, and, therefore, I miss the opportunity for a sale. Such was the case on three previous occasions when I approached a custom-built residence at the east end of community's major street. This time, however, a rather tall brunette in her mid-thirties answered the door and called herself Marilyn. She obviously recognized me by her enthusiastic greeting; and yet, this pretty brunette was only vaguely familiar to me.

Marilyn: Is this book different from the one we bought from you?

Tom: Yes, it is my most recent book.

I was puzzled and stated,

I remember coming to this particular house when I was in this neighbourhood, but each time I arrived nobody was home. Have we met before?

Marilyn: My husband bought your book with the blue cover a number of years ago. It was quite good.

Tom: I am sorry, but I cannot recall him. Could I please have your husband's name?

Marilyn: We are the Davidson family. We lived in the house across the street from you until we finished building this new home.

Tom: That is right. You had a young girl and a newborn. Your face is now registering with me.

Marilyn: Tom, this is the first time you have seen me without the baby fat I accumulated during my pregnancies. I look like a 'new' person since living in your neighbourhood.

Marilyn said it in a way that indicated an expectant response from me.

Tom: You have indeed lost weight.

I then carried on with the conversation.

When you lived in my neighbourhood you also had two large dogs. You drove a turquoise-coloured Oldsmobile Cutless Supreme and your husband's car was a Honda Accord.

Marilyn:	You have excellent memory.
Tom:	People often tell me this.
Marilyn:	I very seldom talked with you, if at all, during our time in your neighbourhood. My husband spoke to you more than I did.
Tom:	You are correct. Our communication consisted only of the customary greetings such as 'hello' and 'have a nice day' from a distance.
Marilyn:	That period of time was very busy for us. I worked shift work in Michigan, had a two-year child and a newborn. At the same time, my husband and I were busy building this home. We were not around enough to establish meaningful relationships with any neighbours.
Tom:	Yes. Your family was always coming and going during your short time in the neighbourhood.
Marilyn:	Both of my children are in school. Life is not quite as hectic as it was when we lived across from you. Let me get the money for your book. Have you been to the house behind mine?
Tom:	I have not made it that far yet this evening.
Marilyn:	My parents live there. I am sure they will buy a book too.
Tom:	Thank you. I will go to your parents' house after I leave here.
Marilyn:	I am happy that you caught me home this evening. It was nice to talk with you.
Tom:	I enjoyed talking to the 'new' you too.

The conversation between Marilyn and me took on an embarrassing tone when she mentioned her reduction in 'baby fat' and her appearance. I did not know how to respond to such a statement, and did not know whether or not I should attempt a rebuttal. I am sure I was blushing throughout the remainder of the presentation after this reference. I find that people's use of words can be very unusual in specific instances.

Tom Cribbin

I dedicate this story to

Fritz & Patti Janssen

PUBLIC PRAYERS

As with most people in my community, the subject of religion and spirituality is a private matter. Generally, individuals respect another person's beliefs regardless of his or her own values and religious background. I have the opinion that each one of us has inherent spiritual qualities. Whenever I meet people as a result of marketing my books, I trust they would conclude I have a strong belief system. However, there are some of my customers who overtly ask me about my religion and church-going habits.

On a late Thursday afternoon I was walking east on Wellington Street to sell my books. I entered a cul-de-sac of eight bungalows and began promoting my latest book to the residents. A woman with short gray hair, whom I estimated to be in her early sixties, greeted me when she took a break from tending to her garden. She said her name was 'Victoria', but indicated that many people call her 'Vicky' and I gave her my name.

Tom: Throughout the past few years, I have written a series of books about dealing with people and my speech difference.

Vicky:	You have probably met many people with differing comments regarding your speech.
Tom:	Yes, I have met all types. Meeting people is always interesting. I even develop stories based on people that I meet when I market my books.
Vicky:	Are people hurtful in their comments about you and your speech?
Tom:	I would use the word 'surprised', rather than 'hurtful'. Since I lived all my life with a speech difference, I think I have developed a rather tough skin for rude and insensitive comments. Having said this, I must always consider the person making the comment. For example, I might be the first person whom he or she has encountered with any sort of speech difference.

I handed Vicki a book to quickly scan, as I needed a break from talking.

Vicky:	Your story titles are quite enticing and rather humourous.
Tom:	I have had many comments from customers saying that my story titles are good. The story titles are perhaps the most difficult aspect of creating the entire book.
Vicky:	How would you characterize your book?
Tom:	As you can see by the story titles, this book will take you on an emotional roller coaster. You will laugh,

you will shake your head in amazement, and you might shed a tear or two. Above all, you will be able to see a variety of human nature behaviours in many of these stories.

Vicky: I would be happy to read your book.

Tom: Thank you.

Vicky went inside her house to retrieve payment for the book and returned with some literature.

Vicky: I would like you to have this literature. It will inspire you.

Tom: I will be certain to read through it.

Vicky: Before you go on your way, would you like to recite 'The Lord's Prayer' with me?

What else could I say, but agree to her request.

There we were together on a late Thursday afternoon, reciting 'The Lord's Prayer' with me sitting on a step as she knelt before me on her front lawn. I always welcome people who pray for me and there is no doubt that we all need prayers. However, I felt uncomfortable and self-conscious to be in receipt of Vicky's prayers in such a public way. I did not want to offend Vicky and her strong religious beliefs, so I recited the prayer with her. I believe a more appropriate response would have been to say, "I will keep you in my daily prayers." Nevertheless, I now consider it an honour and very humbling when customers share their faith with me.

Tom Cribbin

33

I dedicate this story to

Diane Smart

QUESTIONABLE CITIZENSHIP

Since I do not have a car, I rely on friends to drive me to outlying areas where it is impossible for me to walk or I take public transportation to get to my destination. Camlachie is one such community. Bob drove me to Camlachie in his wife's black BMW so I could sell my books that Sunday afternoon in Spring. Camlachie was an area where the residents were not familiar with my books or with me. It was a perfect day for selling books as the weather was sunny and mild. The residents of Camlachie thought the day was ideal for outside activities. When Bob was driving me down King Street, its residents had their eyes peeled on the conspicuous sedan bearing blue, Michigan, license plates. I told Bob that this north-south street should take the majority of the afternoon and I would meet him near the major corner where we entered. He let me out at the opposite end of the street and wished me well.

As I often had done before, I began my brief presentation to the King Street residents with my name, my purpose for being there, and my place of residency. Ted, wearing dark rimmed eyeglasses, was among those who questioned me about my citizenship. He interrupted me when I told him I lived in Sarnia.

Ted firmly stated,

>I know where you live and it is not Sarnia. You live across the Bluewater Bridge in the state of Michigan.

Tom: Why do you say this?

Ted: I noticed the car in which you were riding had blue license plates.

Tom: You are correct in your observation.

Ted: I thought that a person must be a Canadian citizen to work here.

Tom: I will give you an explanation as to why I am riding in a Michigan-plated car.

At this point, Ted could tell that his accusations flustered me. I took a deep breath to calm myself and provided him with a detailed explanation.

>I am a Canadian citizen and I was born in Sarnia. The driver of the black BMW is a great friend of mine, whom I met a few years ago when marketing my book. He and his wife took a liking to me and offered to drive me around the county when they are at their house in Sarnia. The man once worked for Dow at the Canadian head office and finished

his career working for Dow's parent company in Michigan. He and his wife divide their time between Sarnia and Midland, Michigan.

Ted: You are fortunate to have such generous friends.

Tom: I am, indeed, very lucky. There are other good people in our community who have been equally generous to me.

Ted: I accept your explanation and I will take a book off your hands.

Tom: Thank you and enjoy your afternoon.

When Bob arrived to take me back to the city, I told him that his black BMW was the subject of many conversations. People thought I had American citizenship because of the blue Michigan license plate outfitted on the rear of this car. I said sarcastically to Bob, "That is just what I need, a King Street resident to report me to Canada and U.S. Immigration about illegally selling books door-to-door." Anything is possible with the people I meet through the course of selling my book.

Tom Cribbin

I dedicate this story to

Mike & Katherine Caraher

TOM, THE LOST AUTHOR

Mike invited me to Watford, so that I could introduce my latest book and myself to its residents while he attended a business meeting. I had not been to this central Lambton County community in a while prior to this cold and blustery Sunday afternoon. Mike and I agreed upon an approximate time and place to meet a few hours later. Before we went our separate ways, Mike and I mapped out my route of this recently developed subdivision. I dressed in many layers to protect me from the wind. I pulled my royal blue toque — with the words CRIBBIN UNPLUGGED printed across its front — down over my forehead and headed into the cold. Mike gave me his assurance that he would be waiting for me, in his red Dodge Durango, at the intersection of Main and McGregor no later than 2:15 P.M.

I began knocking on doors promoting my book and attempted to keep my presentation as concise as possible given the inclement weather. People were friendly and asked me to step inside to explain my book to them. They had concern for me being out in the blustery weather and I had my own concern regarding the wind gusts that day. Nevertheless, I accepted their genuine concern and carried on with my task of selling the allotted books for the afternoon. The day's miserable weather was the opening line in my presentation for each person I approached. As usual, I would notice items such as hockey gear at the door's entrance way and would engage in a conversation about hockey or other topics. My knack for talking allowed me to stand inside a person's door and to obtain warmth for a few minutes.

I headed onto Victoria Drive and estimated that I could complete this meandering street before my 2:15 ride arrived. I rang the doorbell of a huge yellow bungalow with odd-looking shingles. A man named George answered the door. He, like many of his fellow residents, invited me to come in while I presented him with information about my book. George bought my latest book with little sales effort on my part. Furthermore, I told him of my various speaking engagements and of my three other books. I promoted my website where he could obtain more information about myself. I thanked George for his interest and made my way to the next house on the street.

My next stop was a recently built house at the other end of Victoria. The matriarch of the house was also nice to me and she expressed concern about the day's very frigid weather. I explained to her since it is a sunny day and I am constantly moving, it does not feel that cold. After her house, I walked to the corner and waited for my ride. I waited and waited. Mike's big red fire truck, as he calls his Durango, could not be seen anywhere. I paced up and down Main Street, looking for a pay phone or a glimpse of Mike's Durango. I could not see either one.

I walked back to George's house. I told him that my ride was thirty minutes late and asked him to call Mike on his cell phone to determine his whereabouts. George attempted to reach Mike directly and left this message on Mike's answering service.

> I have a friend of yours — Tom, the author — here in Watford waiting for a ride from you. He is at the yellow bungalow on Victoria Drive. Tom is wondering if your meeting is running late or if you forgot about him. Please call back.

Meanwhile, George had to leave his mother's house to attend to another errand. He allowed me to wait inside until my ride arrived. Before he left, George told me that he would phone Mike every fifteen minutes until Mike answered his cell phone. While I was patiently waiting for Mike, George's gracious mother gave me a cup of warm tea and a piece of cake to satisfy my thirst and hunger.

It seemed like an eternity had passed until Anthony, who I assumed was George's brother, entered his mother's home. Anthony very bluntly asked me what my purpose was for standing in the front hallway of his family's residence. I explained my situation and the fact that his mother and brother invited me into the house until my ride arrived. I gave him Mike's number and this time Mike answered his cell phone. Anthony relayed the message that Mike was only a few minutes away from Victoria Drive. I thanked the men's mother for her hospitality and Anthony walked with me to the edge of the property until the red Durango arrived. Mike apologized to me for being so late. His meeting with his potential clients had gone longer than he had anticipated.

Mike and I were now heading home to Sarnia about 4:00 P.M. when his cell phone rang. It was George, who, according to Mike, sounds identical on the phone to his brother, Anthony. George's query to Mike was, "Have you found Tom, the lost author?" Mike gave the concerned Watford resident a history of my books and my persistence in selling door-to-door. It is my understanding, only from the one side of the telephone conversation, that George respected my effort and enthusiasm when I first met him. I am sure George will enjoy the stories in my latest book and his family will always remember me from that blustery winter day.

Tom Cribbin

I dedicate this story to

Ross & Kim Grant

THE PROVOCATIVE T-SHIRT

One morning I set out to market my books. I headed south on Indian Road, a major thoroughfare in our city, until I reached Oak Avenue. As it was the first balmy day of the spring season, residents were enjoying the sunshine while performing various outdoor chores. I made my way from east to west on Oak Avenue talking with residents about my writing, my cerebral palsy and their varied interests. Many people were both buying my books and praising me for my tenacity. When I go door-to-door, it amazes the potential customer as to what I perceive about the present situation.

I was now approaching the half way mark on Oak Avenue where I could see a Harley Davidson motorcycle parked on a paved driveway about three houses down. I saw the owner when I took a few more steps towards the split-level house. The bald-headed, burly man wore a black T-shirt with the following provocative saying displayed in-large white lettering.

I don't need any more friends

Ordinarily, I would make a judgment call about the total situation and pass on that particular residence. I made the assumption that this man would not have an interest in buying my book but, nevertheless, I approached him to inquire. It is my intention to have many people, from varied backgrounds read, and hopefully enjoy, my stories. So, here I was standing before this man who was adorned in the previously described T-shirt. We greeted each other by exchanging our names. Like many of my potential customers, he introduced himself only by his first name, Fred.

Tom: Your T-shirt sure has a very interesting saying on it.

Fred: It catches people's attention.

Tom: I can just imagine the comments from your neighbours, who have small children, when you wear this shirt.

Fred: My neighbours just smile or shake their head in disgust.

After my brief comment regarding the provocative saying, my focus was now on the second phrase in smaller print.

Tom: I don't necessarily want to be your friend, however, I would like you to buy my book about my life's experiences.

Fred: You are pretty smart to use that in your sales pitch.

Tom: Well Fred, I try to be perceptive about my potential clients and their surroundings.

Fred: I guess the saying on my T-shirt is noticeable.

Tom:	Well, yeah. You don't say!

I allowed Fred to scan the book hoping to entice him into buying a copy.

Fred:	It looks like it would be fun to read. I think I could handle reading your book. I don't usually read a lot. Since you took the time to write the book, then I will make the time to read it. If I buy your book, will you guarantee me that I will have some laughs?
Tom:	I am positive you will have a few hearty chuckles.
Fred:	We have a deal.
Tom:	Here is an autographed copy for your reading enjoyment. Thank you for your time today.

I am just as guilty as the next person for judging an individual based on his or her appearance, however, my perception of some people changes when I speak with them. The burly motorcycle owner and I had an unlikely interesting conversation that Saturday morning. Although Fred had a rather tough personality, as highlighted by his vulgar T-shirt, he demonstrated a willingness to listen to me talk about my book. He invited me back to bring the other books I have written. I would certainly return just to see the message on the T-shirt that Fred might be wearing.

Tom Cribbin

I dedicate this story to

Daniela Azzolina

MR. TOM

Bridlepath Trail is a road consisting of upscale, executive-style homes and spacious bungalows in a newly developed subdivision north of the highway. Well-educated and highly motivated individuals and their families occupy these residences. My strategy for approaching individuals of this upscale neighbourhood was not different from approaching people in other parts of the city and county. My technique for selling my books has been to personalize each presentation to some degree. I would observe something unique to that individual's property and include it into my introduction as I did with Robert, a potential buyer of my book.

I met Robert who was doing chores at the edge of his driveway. I introduced myself by articulating my first and last names slowly and asking him for a few minutes of his time. My next question to him concerned his Infiniti SUV parked in the double car garage.

Tom: Is that a Texas license plate I see on your Infiniti?

Robert: You are correct, Mr. Tom. We moved here about a year ago.

44

From his first few sentences, I noticed his unmistakable southern drawl and made an assumption about his Texas roots.

Robert:	You are not right. I was born in Louisiana and worked in Texas until my transfer to Sarnia.
Tom:	You must work in the petro-chemical industry.
Robert:	Yes, I am in oil. I am working at Exxon-Mobil's subsidiary.
Tom:	And that is, of course, Imperial Oil.

Robert said, "I am in oil", with the same enthusiasm as those characters had in the 1980's television series *Dallas*.

Robert:	You are quite clever to know the connection between Exxon-Mobil and Imperial.
Tom:	It is common knowledge in Sarnia that Exxon has a majority interest in Imperial. How do you like living in Canada?
Robert:	It is a nice country. I liked the fact that the Canadian dollar was worth considerably less in comparison to the US greenback when we bought this house. Now, the Canadian dollar has become closer in value since we moved here.

The conversation then turned to the purpose of my visit to Bridlepath Trail.

Robert:	Can I see what is in your other hand, Mr. Tom?

Tom:	I have written a book about the unusual circumstances I find myself in when I am marketing my books.
Robert:	I am sure you have had some strange experiences with people.
Tom:	In my last two books, I wrote mainly about the naïveté and insensitivity of people about my speech cadence and pronunciation. For example, I had a woman who called the police to report me; another man who thought I was faking my speech difference; and yet another who thought I ought to live in a group home.
Robert:	It must be very frustrating for you, Mr. Tom.
Tom:	Yes it is. The stories in this latest book outline the humourous, interpersonal relationships I have developed with my customers. I can notice the positive attitude change in people since I first appeared on their doorsteps about eight years ago. I always look for the positive in people.
Robert:	Despite your cadence difficulty, I can tell you have a good education. Just wait here as I will go and get the money for your book.
Tom:	Thank you.
Robert:	I look forward to reading your book, Mr. Tom.
Tom:	Have a good laugh while you read it.
Robert:	I will. Take it easy, Mr. Tom.

Robert employed some of his southern politeness when referring to me as 'Mr. Tom'. Although this man and I have very different life experiences, there exists a commonality between us. He and I had an interesting conversation about his employer, the US vs. Canadian currencies, and experiences with my speech cadence. I have learned that when I take an interest in a potential customer's surroundings, then that individual is likely to respond favourably to me.

Tom Cribbin

I dedicate this story to

Joan Ross

HOT CHOCOLATE PERFECTION

I have known Cindy Weathers since I introduced my first book to her some years ago. This general surgeon has been among my loyal customers who have bought my three previous books. As Dr. Weathers has a young family and a busy medical practice, my interactions with her have been brief. Furthermore, even catching her at home for a few minutes to introduce her to my latest book was becoming quite the challenge. After many attempts to reach her during the year, I walked to the doctor's distinctive blue-sided residence on a brisk November afternoon, rang the bell and waited for an answer. Dr. Weathers recognized me immediately and inquired if I had, possibly, written another series of stories for her to enjoy. I confirmed that I had released my fourth book earlier this year and showed her the glossy, artistic cover.

Dr. Weathers purchased a copy for her mother and another one for herself. She explained that her mother had been a nurse in the maternity ward and she was familiar with cerebral palsy. After Cindy and I completed the transaction, she asked me if I would like a cup of hot chocolate on this cold afternoon. I accepted her kind gesture.

While Cindy was in the kitchen making the hot chocolate treat, I sat at her dining room table. She made the hot chocolate differently from the way I make it at my house. I make hot chocolate the "lazy man's way" by heating water in the kettle and stirring the pre-mixed packages into a cup. Cindy prepares her hot chocolate by heating milk and adding chocolate syrup to satisfy one's taste. The doctor returned to the dining room with a bowl of fruit and indicated that the milk was on low heat and we began our chat.

Dr. Weathers and I had a thoughtful, meaningful conversation intertwined with lighter moments. I discussed aspects of my life that I rarely, if at all, talk about with even the closest of friends; let alone the readers of my books. Cindy told me that I deserved much credit for going door-to-door to educate people and to sell my books.

Dr. Weathers was surprised when I told her that I give talks to students about the social aspect of having a disability. She was glad that I enjoy a positive response from the students. She asked me whether her medical brethren were supporters of my books. "Most people in the health care profession have occasionally bought my books," I replied.

Cindy returned to the kitchen to prepare my hot milk and the chocolate syrup. She then returned to the dining room and said, "Unfortunately, there is only a small amount of chocolate syrup. Tom, this is quite embarrassing! Anyway, please go ahead and see if it requires more chocolate." Being polite, I commented that it tasted good. Cindy took a sip from her cup and determined both of our cups required much more chocolate.

Since Dr. Weathers did not have any more syrup, she would need to improvise by performing a chemistry experiment with the heated milk. She added some Fry's Cocoa, used in baking cakes, to the cups of hot chocolate. Cindy warned me that adding this type of baking product to the hot chocolate would not taste too great. I quickly consoled her and I commented, "If I get sick, then I am in the company of the right person as you are a doctor." She returned my comment with, "You will not be physically sick from my hot chocolate, but it will leave a very bitter taste in your mouth." I sipped a tiny amount and my facial expression indicated to Dr. Weathers that my hot chocolate needed some sweetener. Sensing that I might find the hot chocolate bitter, the doctor already had the bag of sugar on the table. She kept pouring sugar into my cup until the taste satisfied my palate. When the hot chocolate finally tasted delicious to me, Dr. Weathers completed her chemistry experiment of heated milk, syrup, Fry's Cocoa, and sugar with perfection.

It was gracious of Dr. Weathers to spend so much time with me on that cold November afternoon. She had been a loyal reader of my books, and now a respectful friendship has developed.

Tom Cribbin

I dedicate this story to

Janet Coker

PEOPLE DON'T GET IT

Although I have established a loyal following of my books, I am always seeking new customers. I still receive odd questions from potential customers, as I did when I began marketing my books many years ago. While the majority of people understand that selling my book is a way for me to support myself, some people *just don't get it*. I can remember two such instances where the individuals should have understood this intent.

I walked to an outdoor shopping plaza and began marketing my latest book to the offices above the retail establishments. Most workers in the offices had become familiar with my books and myself during the last few years. These were among the first workplaces I contact with any new book. As with many buildings, this building had new tenants not familiar with my books. The Lambton Charitable Society, a local philanthropic organization, was one such tenant.

I entered the Lambton Charitable Society's office and patiently waited until the woman, seated before me, finished her telephone call. While she was on the phone, I took my information, along with a book, to show her. The auburn haired woman introduced herself as Patricia, the Executive Director.

I introduced myself by placing information about my book on Patricia's desk for her review while I told her about myself. The entrance wall had portraits of the society's board of directors. As part of my introduction to Patricia I indicated that selected board members had previously bought and enjoyed my books. This strategy of mentioning individuals to the potential customer proved beneficial in generating sales for me. Patricia nodded her approval with the provided information, and then another telephone call came into the Lambton Charitable Society. While she was on the phone for the second time, I placed a copy of my latest book on her desk. After her brief call, Patricia thanked me for the copy of the book. I said to her, "Don't put the book away too quickly. There is a cost associated with the book." Patricia had a look of astonishment on her face. I told her that she could buy my book at the bookstore at the other side of the shopping plaza or on-line. I promptly took the CRIBBIN UNPLUGGED book off her desk, thanked her for the time, and exited her office.

About a month after my encounter with Patricia, I marketed the latest book in a new residential development across from the local college. Since I had never been in this subdivision, I focused on enunciating every word while maintaining good eye contact with the potential customer. Residents made me feel very comfortable as I attempted to sell my book. I had many interesting questions from the people of these three or four streets. I complimented those who asked me thoughtful and empathetic questions, and, in return, I did my best to provide them with just as thoughtful answers. However, among the residents was a woman in her early thirties with long brown hair named Deirdre. Her question was anything but astute. As with other residents in this neighbourhood, I spent considerable time with Deirdre introducing my book, its characteristics and some personal background. Then, Deirdre asked me a rather insulting question, "Is there a cost for this book?" I responded by calmly saying, "Yes, there is a cost." She then handed the book back to me. Some people do not realize that I publish the books and that I sell my work for a living.

Many potential customers have asked me, "What is the asking price for your book?" Once told, it is the potential customer's decision either to accept or deny the asking price. As for Deirdre's question, I am not writing and publishing books just for something to do. I have an interesting way of story telling and I offer my book at a fair price to people.

Both Patricia and Deirdre surprised me with similar reactions to my book. I wonder whether Patricia or Deirdre would have asked another person such a ludicrous question. I suspect not. First, knocking on doors selling a book is itself unorthodox in today's society, but moreover, it is still uncommon in some people's minds to see and hear a person such as myself selling a self-authored book. Patricia and Deirdre witnessed, as my family and friends have known for years, that I do things in an unconventional manner.

Tom Cribbin

I dedicate this story to

Victoria Hastie

MAINTAINING SCHOOL STANDARDS

Gary is often one of the first people I contact regarding any new book of mine. I have known Gary and his siblings my entire life as we lived in the same neighbourhood. I telephoned Gary to inform him that the release of my fourth book would be in early April. Also, I told him about my impending website promoting all my books.

As Gary and I were talking on the phone, I could hear his daughter in the background relaying a message to me via her dad.

Gary: My daughter tells me that her school has three of your books on display in the library.

Tom: I am glad to say that most of the elementary schools have at least one of my books in their libraries. I have heard that your children attend one of the top-rated schools in the country.

Gary: It is quite the honour given to Gregory A. Hogan School. The parents knew of this honour for some time. The children of the school scored a very high percentile on the provincial testing system. The teachers' dedication to their profession and to their students at Gregory Hogan is excellent.

Tom: I have my own theory as to why the school is one of the ten best.

Gary: Tell me your theory Tom.

I said, with my tongue firmly planted in my cheek, that

the mere presence of my books in Gregory Hogan School must have given the students added inspiration to obtain high marks.

Gary said laughingly,

That is as good an explanation as I have heard.

Tom: Actually it was Steve, our childhood neighbour, who had bought my first book when he was the principal of Gregory Hogan School.

Gary: That must have been an easy sale for you to make.

Tom: Knowing Steve and having him as a principal made it a whole lot easier for me to introduce my books to other schools. Your neighbour, the lawyer who married a dentist, bought a set of my books for her daughter's classroom. Your children might have seen my books in a class as well as in the library.

Gary: We know the lawyer and her family quite well. My daughter mentioned that your books are in her class this year.

Tom:	Last year, I sold a copy of my CRIBBIN UNPLUGGED book to the most recent principal of Gregory A. Hogan School.
Gary:	We had two or three principals since my children have been attending the school. All of the principals have been excellent. Is Steve still a principal or has he moved into administration?
Tom:	Steve was the principal of St. Anne's school last year. He has since retired from the school board.
Gary:	That's right! My brother has not seen Steve on various teacher-parent nights this year at his children's school. Well, Tom, I should be on my way. My daughter wants me to take her to the mall for some supplies for a school project.
Tom:	In that case, I won't keep you any longer. I want your children to maintain the high standards when the next provincial testing comes around.
Gary:	Oh, yeah! We must maintain those high standards. Talk with you later.

Both elementary and secondary school principals were very receptive to the message I conveyed in my books. As one educator said to me jokingly, "Every time I see you, I know it is time to get out my wallet and buy a book."

I have known Gary since I was very young. Gary and his siblings have been close friends throughout my life. I am positive that his brothers and sisters have shared humourous and offbeat stories with their children about growing up with me.

Tom Cribbin

I dedicate this story to

Larry & Josie Parker

A DOUBTING PROFESSIONAL

Lakeview Lane is an exclusive street situated between Lake Huron and Lakeshore Road. Approximately half the street is private, meaning the residents are responsible for routine services such as snow removal. I had been to Lakeview Lane to market my books previously at which time I addressed the 'PRIVATE BEYOND THIS POINT' sign with a customer. The resident assured me I had the right to market my books to the houses on the private end of the street. When I release a book, Lakeview Lane has been a favourite street to start marketing any new book. I often have one other book title with me to sell to people who may not have been home during my last visit.

On a weekend afternoon, my regular customers warmly welcomed me when I introduced my latest book to them. Mrs. Hillsdale, a regular customer, said to me that I should continue to do well selling my book as most of the same people remain as residents. I thanked her for the information and proceeded with confidence to the next house. She was correct in that many people immediately recognized me and quickly bought my latest book.

I was brimming with confidence when I introduced myself to John Carling, whose tone, I would soon discover, matched his abrupt personality. Following suit, I became very serious. He began with this statement,

> We, the residents of this street, do not appreciate people door-to-door soliciting. It is an exclusive part of the city. Are you a natural gas reseller?

Tom: I am not a gas reseller.

My confidence waned at the tone of John's voice. I reassured John of my purpose for being on this street and began naming some of its residents. I asked John if he would like to see a copy of my book. While he reviewed my book, I told him more about my other books and myself. My focus then shifted to his sports car, an AUDI A4.

Tom: I really like your car!

John: I like it, too.

Tom: I have only seen two A4's in Sarnia, a black one and a green one. I always see a black one, similar to yours, parked in the doctor's parking lot on Mitton Street.

John smiled and said,

> You are very observant. My car is the black one you see parked in the doctor's lot. I am a physician.

	I have a clinic in the hospital. Please don't address me as 'Doctor...' I am not your doctor.
Tom:	Since you are a doctor, you have some knowledge of cerebral palsy.
John:	I have limited knowledge, although I had no specific training in the topic. You would have more knowledge on the condition than I do.
Tom:	It is refreshing to hear this admission from a doctor. My books are about the reactions of people to my speech difference. I must say some reactions have been comical while others have been very rude.
John:	I will buy your book. You said this is your latest book. Do you have other books with you?
Tom:	I have my first book with me.
John:	I will take your first book and your latest book.
Tom:	Here are autographed copies of my books. I sign them at home because my writing is quite illegible just like many doctors.
John:	You are correct in saying that doctors have poor penmanship. I will enjoy reading about your adventures.
Tom:	Thank you for your time today.

John was abrupt at the beginning of our brief meeting, but after he learned about my history of selling books in his exclusive neighbourhood, his abruptness disappeared. I think I impressed John with my education, my achievements, and, yes, my astute observations. When a person drives an AUDI A4, with customized plates, it is easy for anyone to notice that car. Once I left John's property, I brimmed with confidence again having sold two of my books to a difficult person.

Tom Cribbin

I dedicate this story to

Laura Bubola

A PLEASANT AWAKENING

A tradition dating back to the early 1980's is the annual naming of individuals and organizations to the Mayor's Honour List for the City of Sarnia. The mayor's office releases the list a few days prior to the year's end with a forthcoming reception for the honourees in the New Year. While I like to hear the names of the honourees every year, I really only took a fleeting interest in the honour. In most years, I recognized the honourees by name only.

After arriving home late one evening, I struggled to awaken at my usual time of 6:30 A.M. I pressed the snooze button a few times and, in my sleep, I heard a local news reporter utter, "Headlining news for this hour is the release of the Mayor's Honour List by Mike Bradley. Among the individuals who made this year's list is Tom Cribbin, .a local author with a speech disability caused by cerebral palsy." Wow, I could not believe that I made the Mayor's Honour List by just writing and selling books. The announcement of this news prompted me to rise for the day.

That day, I received many congratulatory wishes about the prestigious honour from family and friends. Paddy, a close friend with a remarkable sense of humour, called me and said, "Congratulations Tom. I have read about you in the newspapers over the past few months. Now, it is just getting ridiculous when I hear your name on the radio as I wake up. You are all over the local media." After her good-natured ribbing, Paddy asked me with much enthusiasm, "When did you learn about your selection to the Mayor's Honour List?" "I learned that my name was on the Honour List as you had through the local media," I told her. She was surprised that I had no advance knowledge of the honour.

As the award ceremony drew near, I decided on my guest list. Among my six allotted guests that accompanied me to the award ceremony were Paddy and her husband, Peter, along with Maggie and her husband, Bob. My friendship with Paddy developed over the last several years as we do our errands together. Paddy's caring nature is especially evident as she remembers days of significance in my life. I have known Maggie since we were classmates in the Business Program at Lambton College in the early 1980's. Bob and Maggie can appreciate my everyday challenges and successes as they have a special needs child. Those two couples have been extraordinarily generous and gracious to me over the past few years. Also, on my guest list were Tom and Krystal, who serve as editors for my books. Tom's tutelage, guidance, and editorial expertise towards my writing have been immeasurable. Krystal is the first person I call concerning any story ideas. When I discuss an idea for a new story with Krystal, her reaction, expressed with her distinct intonation, indicates if the idea is feasible. My guests were very much representative of all the people who have helped me in my life.

After everybody in the reception hall had some hors d'oeuvres, the mayor started the main part of the evening. In his opening remarks, Mr. Bradley indicated that honouring individuals in the community is among his favourite evenings as Mayor. This evening is not about politics but it is a celebration of the people who make Sarnia a special community. There is one basic rule applicable to the Mayor's Honour List: an individual does not ask to be on the list. Citizens contact the Office of the Mayor, citing extraordinary works by particular individuals in the community. A secret committee makes the final selection for the Mayor's Honour List each year. Mr. Bradley clarified that there exists an element of surprise when he releases the Honour List to the press. The nominees and the general public simultaneously learn of the names on the Mayor's Honour List.

Following the history of the award, Mr. Bradley began inviting the nominated individuals or organizations, one-by-one, to the stage to accept their plaques. The mayor gave a personal anecdote of each nominee and, in return, the recipient gave a brief acceptance speech after receiving the plaque. As I sat listening to the mayor's anecdotes and recipients' speeches, I thought my contribution of writing books paled in comparison to the other honoured recipients. I became increasingly more apprehensive as Mr. Bradley called on individuals to accept their plaques for one reason: my time for addressing the hall full of people was drawing near. My guests could also tell I was nervous about talking to the crowd. Paddy gave me her advice, which was, "Visualize you are selling your book at the door to a person and you will talk just fine."

Eventually, our long-serving Mayor began his emotional introduction of me. "I have known Tom Cribbin since the late 1980's, even before I became mayor. We worked on a political campaign together. He writes, publishes and sells books about his experiences with having cerebral palsy. Tom has a business degree from the University of Windsor." The crowd laughed when Mr. Bradley jokingly said, "When Tom enters my office with a recently-penned book; he always exits with some of my money." Additionally, the mayor said that while many of us find Tom's disability to be a major challenge, Tom handles his situation well.

The mayor welcomed me to the microphone for my acceptance speech. Before I had an opportunity to talk, I was overwhelmed by the assembled crowd's ovation. I did not have a prepared speech, so I talked off-the-cuff. I acknowledged each of my six guests individually for his or her friendship and assistance. I ended my speech by thanking my sister, who lives in Ottawa, as well as paying homage to my late parents. When I returned to my seat, I received congratulations about my delivery of the heart-felt speech from my guests. "I think I was smart to remind you of my visualization trick when you delivered your speech," Paddy modestly said to me when discussing that evening some years later. Other friends and I concur with her assessment.

The reception ceremony for the Mayor's Honour List was an emotional evening for my invited guests and for me. I did not realize the impact I had on people until I received that great ovation from the audience. The introduction by the mayor and the ovation were both humbling and unforgettable. Now, when the Mayor's office releases the Honour List, I pay close attention to the individuals or organizations that are bestowed this award.

Tom Cribbin

FINAL THOUGHTS

I have enjoyed meeting each person throughout the marketing of my books. "You have a positive impact on people whether or not you realize it," a woman once said after I sold her one of my books. Before that, I had never thought about the impact I had on people when they first meet me.

My life is remarkably similar to the lives of other people. Most individuals I meet understand this point, whereas some people will never understand this fact. As I said in one story, my parents and sister did not believe in pampering me because of my disability. Moreover, I described instances with my friends where my cerebral palsy did not prevent me from playing road hockey or climbing the Statue of Liberty.

Once people listen to me or read my stories, they will hopefully conclude that I always project a positive image of my different physical characteristics. People's perceptions and attitudes of my speech difference will not restrict me from carrying on with my life's goals.

Tom Cribbin